A DOLL'S HOUSE

Henrik Ibsen

TECHNICAL DIRECTOR Maxwell Krohn
EDITORIAL DIRECTOR Justin Kestler
MANAGING EDITOR Ben Florman

SERIES EDITORS Boomie Aglietti, Justin Kestler
PRODUCTION Christian Lorentzen

WRITERS G. J. Gillis, Jen Westhagen
EDITORS Sarah Friedberg, Dennis Quinio

This edition published by Spark Publishing

Spark Publishing
A Division of SparkNotes LLC
120 Fifth Avenue, 8th Floor
New York, NY 10011

02 03 04 05 SN 9 8 7 6 5 4 3 2 1

Please send all comments and questions or report errors to
feedback@sparknotes.com.

Library of Congress information available upon request

Printed and bound in the United States

RRD-C

ISBN 1-58663-459-3

Introduction: Stopping to Buy Sparknotes on a Snowy Evening

Whose words these are you *think* you know.
Your paper's due tomorrow, though;
We're glad to see you stopping here
To get some help before you go.

Lost your course? You'll find it here.
Face tests and essays without fear.
Between the words, good grades at stake:
Get great results throughout the year.

Once school bells caused your heart to quake
As teachers circled each mistake.
Use SparkNotes and no longer weep,
Ace every single test you take.

Yes, books are lovely, dark, and deep,
But only what you grasp you keep,
With hours to go before you sleep,
With hours to go before you sleep.

CONTENTS

NOTE: This SparkNote refers to Frank McGuinness's translation of *A Doll's House*, published by Faber and Faber in 1996. The spelling of character names may differ in other translations of the play.

Context

H ENRIK IBSEN, considered by many to be the father of modern prose drama, was born in Skien, Norway, on March 20, 1828. He was the second of six children. Ibsen's father was a prominent merchant, but he went bankrupt when Ibsen was eight years old, so Ibsen spent much of his early life living in poverty. From 1851 to 1864, he worked in theaters in Bergen and in what is now Oslo (then called Christiania). At age twenty-one, Ibsen wrote his first play, a five-act tragedy called *Catiline*. Like much of his early work, *Catiline* was written in verse.

In 1858, Ibsen married Suzannah Thoreson, and eventually had one son with her. Ibsen felt that, rather than merely live together, husband and wife should live as equals, free to become their own human beings. (This belief can be seen clearly in *A Doll's House*.) Consequently, Ibsen's critics attacked him for failing to respect the institution of marriage. Like his private life, Ibsen's writing tended to stir up sensitive social issues, and some corners of Norwegian society frowned upon his work. Sensing criticism in Oslo about not only his work but also his private life, Ibsen moved to Italy in 1864 with the support of a traveling grant and a stipend from the Norwegian government. He spent the next twenty-seven years living abroad, mostly in Italy and Germany.

Ibsen's early years as a playwright were not lucrative, but he did gain valuable experience during this time. In 1866, Ibsen published his first major theatrical success, a lyric drama called *Brand*. He followed it with another well-received verse play, *Peer Gynt*. These two works helped solidify Ibsen's reputation as one of the premier Norwegian dramatists of his era. In 1879, while living in Italy, Ibsen published his masterpiece, *A Doll's House*. Unlike *Peer Gynt* and *Brand*, *A Doll's House* was written in prose. It is widely considered a landmark in the development of what soon became a highly prevalent genre of theater—realism, which strives to portray life accurately and shuns idealized visions of it. In *A Doll's House*, Ibsen employs the themes and structures of classical tragedy while writing in prose about everyday, unexceptional people. *A Doll's House* also manifests Ibsen's concern for women's rights, and for human rights in general.

Ibsen followed *A Doll's House* with two additional plays written in an innovative, realistic mode: *Ghosts,* in 1881, and *An Enemy of the People,* in 1882. Both were successes. Ibsen began to gain international recognition, and his works were produced across Europe and translated into many different languages.

In his later work, Ibsen moved away from realistic drama to tackle questions of a psychological and subconscious nature. Accordingly, symbols began to gain prominence in his plays. Among the works he wrote in this symbolist period are *The Wild Duck* (1884) and *Hedda Gabler* (1890). *Hedda Gabler* was the last play Ibsen wrote while living abroad. In 1891, he returned to Oslo. His later dramas include *The Master Builder* (1892) and *Little Eyolf* (1896). Eventually, a crippling sickness afflicted Ibsen and prevented him from writing. He died on May 23, 1906.

A NOTE ON THE TITLE

Though most English translations of the play are titled *A Doll's House,* some scholars believe that "A Doll House" is a more accurate translation of the original Norwegian. They feel that it is more suggestive of the doll-like qualities of the entire cast of characters. This SparkNote preserves the more common title—*A Doll's House*—for consistency.

Plot Overview

A DOLL'S HOUSE opens on Christmas Eve. Nora Helmer enters her well-furnished living room—the setting of the entire play—carrying several packages. Torvald Helmer, Nora's husband, comes out of his study when he hears her arrive. He greets her playfully and affectionately, but then chides her for spending so much money on Christmas gifts. Their conversation reveals that the Helmers have had to be careful with money for many years, but that Torvald has recently obtained a new position at the bank where he works that will afford them a more comfortable lifestyle.

Helene, the maid, announces that the Helmers' dear friend Dr. Rank has come to visit. At the same time, another visitor has arrived, this one unknown. To Nora's great surprise, Kristine Linde, a former school friend, comes into the room. The two have not seen each other for years, but Nora mentions having read that Mrs. Linde's husband passed away a few years earlier. Mrs. Linde tells Nora that when her husband died, she was left with no money and no children. Nora tells Mrs. Linde about her first year of marriage to Torvald. She explains that they were very poor and both had to work long hours. Torvald became sick, she adds, and the couple had to travel to Italy so that Torvald could recover.

Nora inquires further about Mrs. Linde's life, and Mrs. Linde explains that for years she had to care for her sick mother and her two younger brothers. She states that her mother has passed away, though, and that the brothers are too old to need her. Instead of feeling relief, Mrs. Linde says she feels empty because she has no occupation; she hopes that Torvald may be able to help her obtain employment. Nora promises to speak to Torvald and then reveals a great secret to Mrs. Linde—without Torvald's knowledge, Nora illegally borrowed money for the trip that she and Torvald took to Italy; she told Torvald that the money had come from her father. For years, Nora reveals, she has worked and saved in secret, slowly repaying the debt, and soon it will be fully repaid.

Krogstad, a low-level employee at the bank where Torvald works, arrives and proceeds into Torvald's study. Nora reacts uneasily to Krogstad's presence, and Dr. Rank, coming out of the study, says Krogstad is "morally sick." Once he has finished meeting with Krogstad, Torvald comes into the living room and says that he can probably hire Mrs. Linde at the bank. Dr. Rank, Torvald, and Mrs. Linde then depart, leaving Nora by herself. Nora's children return with their nanny, Anne-Marie, and Nora plays with them until she notices Krogstad's presence in the room. The two converse, and Krogstad is revealed to be the source of Nora's secret loan.

Krogstad states that Torvald wants to fire him from his position at the bank and alludes to his own poor reputation. He asks Nora to use her influence to ensure that his position remains secure. When she refuses, Krogstad points out that he has in his possession a contract that contains Nora's forgery of her father's signature. Krogstad blackmails Nora, threatening to reveal her crime and to bring shame and disgrace on both Nora and her husband if she does not prevent Torvald from firing him. Krogstad leaves, and when Torvald returns, Nora tries to convince him not to fire Krogstad, but Torvald will hear nothing of it. He declares Krogstad an immoral man and states that he feels physically ill in the presence of such people.

Act Two opens on the following day, Christmas. Alone, Nora paces her living room, filled with anxiety. Mrs. Linde arrives and helps sew Nora's costume for the ball that Nora will be attending at her neighbors' home the following evening. Nora tells Mrs. Linde that Dr. Rank has a mortal illness that he inherited from his father. Nora's suspicious behavior leads Mrs. Linde to guess that Dr. Rank is the source of Nora's loan. Nora denies Mrs. Linde's charge but refuses to reveal the source of her distress. Torvald arrives, and Nora again begs him to keep Krogstad employed at the bank, but again Torvald refuses. When Nora presses him, he admits that Krogstad's moral behavior isn't all that bothers him—he dislikes Krogstad's overly familiar attitude. Torvald and Nora argue until Torvald sends the maid to deliver Krogstad's letter of dismissal.

Torvald leaves. Dr. Rank arrives and tells Nora that he knows he is close to death. She attempts to cheer him up and begins to flirt with him. She seems to be preparing to ask him to intervene on her behalf in her struggle with Torvald. Suddenly, Dr. Rank reveals to Nora that he is in love with her. In light of this revelation, Nora refuses to ask Dr. Rank for anything.

Once Dr. Rank leaves, Krogstad arrives and demands an explanation for his dismissal. He wants respectability and has changed the terms of the blackmail: he now insists to Nora that not only that he be rehired at the bank but that he be rehired in a higher position. He then puts a letter detailing Nora's debt and forgery in the

Helmers' letterbox. In a panic, Nora tells Mrs. Linde everything, and Mrs. Linde instructs Nora to delay Torvald from opening the letter as long as possible while she goes to speak with Krogstad. In order to distract Torvald from the letterbox, Nora begins to practice the tarantella she will perform at that evening's costume party. In her agitated emotional state, she dances wildly and violently, displeasing Torvald. Nora manages to make Torvald promise not to open his mail until after she performs at the party. Mrs. Linde soon returns and says that she has left Krogstad a note but that he will be gone until the following evening.

The next night, as the costume party takes place upstairs, Krogstad meets Mrs. Linde in the Helmers' living room. Their conversation reveals that the two had once deeply in love, but Mrs. Linde left Krogstad for a wealthier man who would enable her to support her family. She tells Krogstad that now that she is free of her own familial obligations and wishes to be with Krogstad and care for his children. Krogstad is overjoyed and says he will demand his letter back before Torvald can read it and learn Nora's secret. Mrs. Linde, however, insists he leave the letter, because she believes both Torvald and Nora will be better off once the truth has been revealed.

Soon after Krogstad's departure, Nora and Torvald enter, back from the costume ball. After saying goodnight to Mrs. Linde, Torvald tells Nora how desirable she looked as she danced. Dr. Rank, who was also at the party and has come to say goodnight, promptly interrupts Torvald's advances on Nora. After Dr. Rank leaves, Torvald finds in his letterbox two of Dr. Rank's visiting cards, each with a black cross above the name. Nora knows Dr. Rank's cards constitute his announcement that he will soon die, and she informs Torvald of this fact. She then insists that Torvald read Krogstad's letter.

Torvald reads the letter and is outraged. He calls Nora a hypocrite and a liar and complains that she has ruined his happiness. He declares that she will not be allowed to raise their children. Helene then brings in a letter. Torvald opens it and discovers that Krogstad has returned Nora's contract (which contains the forged signature). Overjoyed, Torvald attempts to dismiss his past insults, but his harsh words have triggered something in Nora. She declares that despite their eight years of marriage, they do not understand one another. Torvald, Nora asserts, has treated her like a "doll" to be played with and admired. She decides to leave Torvald, declaring that she must "make sense of [her]self and everything around her." She walks out, slamming the door behind her.

CHARACTER LIST

In some editions of A Doll's House, *the speech prompts refer to the character of Torvald Helmer as "Torvald;" in others, they refer to him as "Helmer." Similarly, in some editions, Mrs. Linde's first name is spelled "Christine" rather than "Kristine."*

Nora   The protagonist of the play and the wife of Torvald Helmer. Nora initially seems like a playful, naïve child who lacks knowledge of the world outside her home. She does have some worldly experience, however, and the small acts of rebellion in which she engages indicate that she is not as innocent or happy as she appears. She comes to see her position in her marriage with increasing clarity and finds the strength to free herself from her oppressive situation.

Torvald Helmer Nora's husband. Torvald delights in his new position at the bank, just as he delights in his position of authority as a husband. He treats Nora like a child, in a manner that is both kind and patronizing. He does not view Nora as an equal but rather as a plaything or doll to be teased and admired. In general, Torvald is overly concerned with his place and status in society, and he allows his emotions to be swayed heavily by the prospect of society's respect and the fear of society's scorn.

Krogstad A lawyer who went to school with Torvald and holds a subordinate position at Torvald's bank. Krogstad's character is contradictory: though his bad deeds seem to stem from a desire to protect his children from scorn, he is perfectly willing to use unethical tactics to achieve his goals. His willingness to allow Nora to suffer is despicable, but his claims to feel sympathy for her and the hard circumstances of his own life compel us to sympathize with him to some degree.

Mrs. Linde Nora's childhood friend. Kristine Linde is a practical, down-to-earth woman, and her sensible worldview highlights Nora's somewhat childlike outlook on life. Mrs. Linde's account of her life of poverty underscores the privileged nature of the life that Nora leads. Also, we learn that Mrs. Linde took responsibility for her sick parent, whereas Nora abandoned her father when he was ill.

Dr. Rank Torvald's best friend. Dr. Rank stands out as the one character in the play who is by and large unconcerned with what others think of him. He is also notable for his stoic acceptance of his fate. Unlike Torvald and Nora, Dr. Rank admits to the diseased nature (literally, in his case) of his life. For the most part, he avoids talking to Torvald about his imminent death out of respect for Torvald's distaste for ugliness.

Bob, Emmy, and Ivar Nora and Torvald's three small children. In her brief interaction with her children, Nora shows herself to be a loving mother. When she later refuses to spend time with her children because she fears she may morally corrupt them, Nora acts on her belief that the quality of parenting strongly influences a child's development.

Anne-Marie The Helmers' nanny. Though Ibsen doesn't fully develop her character, Anne-Marie seems to be a kindly woman who has genuine affection for Nora. She had to give up her own daughter in order to take the nursing job offered by Nora's father. Thus, she shares with Nora and Mrs. Linde the act of sacrificing her own happiness out of economic necessity.

Nora's father Though Nora's father is dead before the action of the play begins, the characters refer to him throughout the play. Though she clearly loves and admires her father, Nora also comes to blame him for contributing to her subservient position in life.

ANALYSIS OF MAJOR CHARACTERS

NORA HELMER

At the beginning of *A Doll's House*, Nora seems completely happy. She responds affectionately to Torvald's teasing, speaks with excitement about the extra money his new job will provide, and takes pleasure in the company of her children and friends. She does not seem to mind her doll-like existence, in which she is coddled, pampered, and patronized.

As the play progresses, Nora reveals that she is not just a "silly girl," as Torvald calls her. That she understands the business details related to the debt she incurred taking out a loan to preserve Torvald's health indicates that she is intelligent and possesses capacities beyond mere wifehood. Her description of her years of secret labor undertaken to pay off her debt shows her fierce determination and ambition. Additionally, the fact that she was willing to break the law in order to ensure Torvald's health shows her courage.

Krogstad's blackmail and the trauma that follows do not change Nora's nature; they open her eyes to her unfulfilled and underappreciated potential. "I have been performing tricks for you, Torvald," she says during her climactic confrontation with him. Nora comes to realize that in addition to her literal dancing and singing tricks, she has been putting on a show throughout her marriage. She has pretended to be someone she is not in order to fulfill the role that Torvald, her father, and society at large have expected of her.

Torvald's severe and selfish reaction after learning of Nora's deception and forgery is the final catalyst for Nora's awakening. But even in the first act, Nora shows that she is not totally unaware that her life is at odds with her true personality. She defies Torvald in small yet meaningful ways—by eating macaroons and then lying to him about it, for instance. She also swears, apparently just for the pleasure she derives from minor rebellion against societal standards. As the drama unfolds, and as Nora's awareness of the truth about her life grows, her need for rebellion escalates, culminating in her walking out on her husband and children to find independence.

TORVALD HELMER

Torvald embraces the belief that a man's role in marriage is to protect and guide his wife. He clearly enjoys the idea that Nora needs his guidance, and he interacts with her as a father would. He instructs her with trite, moralistic sayings, such as: "A home that depends on loans and debt is not beautiful because it is not free." He is also eager to teach Nora the dance she performs at the costume party. Torvald likes to envision himself as Nora's savior, asking her after the party, "[D]o you know that I've often wished you were facing some terrible dangers so that I could risk life and limb, risk everything, for your sake?"

Although Torvald seizes the power in his relationship with Nora and refers to her as a "girl," it seems that Torvald is actually the weaker and more childlike character. Dr. Rank's explanation for not wanting Torvald to enter his sickroom—"Torvald is so fastidious, he cannot face up to anything ugly"—suggests that Dr. Rank feels Torvald must be sheltered like a child from the realities of the world. Furthermore, Torvald reveals himself to be childishly petty at times. His real objection to working with Krogstad stems not from deficiencies in Krogstad's moral character but, rather, Krogstad's overly friendly and familiar behavior. Torvald's decision to fire Krogstad stems ultimately from the fact that he feels threatened and offended by Krogstad's failure to pay him the proper respect.

Torvald is very conscious of other people's perceptions of him and of his standing in the community. His explanation for rejecting Nora's request that Krogstad be kept on at the office—that retaining Krogstad would make him "a laughing stock before the entire staff"—shows that he prioritizes his reputation over his wife's desires. Torvald further demonstrates his deep need for society's respect in his reaction to Nora's deception. Although he says that Nora has ruined his happiness and will not be allowed to raise the children, he insists that she remain in the house because his chief concern is saving "the appearance" of their household.

KROGSTAD

Krogstad is the antagonist in *A Doll's House,* but he is not necessarily a villain. Though his willingness to allow Nora's torment to continue is cruel, Krogstad is not without sympathy for her. As he says,

"Even money-lenders, hacks, well, a man like me, can have a little of what you call feeling, you know." He visits Nora to check on her, and he discourages her from committing suicide. Moreover, Krogstad has reasonable motives for behaving as he does: he wants to keep his job at the bank in order to spare his children from the hardships that come with a spoiled reputation. Unlike Torvald, who seems to desire respect for selfish reasons, Krogstad desires it for his family's sake.

Like Nora, Krogstad is a person who has been wronged by society, and both Nora and Krogstad have committed the same crime: forgery of signatures. Though he did break the law, Krogstad's crime was relatively minor, but society has saddled him with the stigma of being a criminal and prohibited him from moving beyond his past. Additionally, Krogstad's claim that his immoral behavior began when Mrs. Linde abandoned him for a man with money so she could provide for her family makes it possible for us to understand Krogstad as a victim of circumstances. One could argue that society forced Mrs. Linde away from Krogstad and thus prompted his crime. Though society's unfair treatment of Krogstad does not justify his actions, it does align him more closely with Nora and therefore tempers our perception of him as a despicable character.

CHARACTER ANALYSIS

THEMES, MOTIFS & SYMBOLS

THEMES

Themes are the fundamental and often universal ideas explored in a literary work.

THE SACRIFICIAL ROLE OF WOMEN

In *A Doll's House,* Ibsen paints a bleak picture of the sacrificial role held by women of all economic classes in his society. In general, the play's female characters exemplify Nora's assertion (spoken to Torvald in Act Three) that even though men refuse to sacrifice their integrity, "hundreds of thousands of women have." In order to support her mother and two brothers, Mrs. Linde found it necessary to abandon Krogstad, her true—but penniless—love, and marry a richer man. The nanny had to abandon her own child to support herself by working as Nora's (and then as Nora's children's) caretaker. As she tells Nora, the nanny considers herself lucky to have found the job, since she was "a poor girl who'd been led astray."

Though Nora is economically advantaged in comparison to the play's other female characters, she nevertheless leads a difficult life because society dictates that Torvald be the marriage's dominant partner. Torvald issues decrees and condescends to Nora, and Nora must hide her loan from him because she knows Torvald could never accept the idea that his wife (or any other woman) had helped save his life. Furthermore, she must work in secret to pay off her loan because it is illegal for a woman to obtain a loan without her husband's permission. By motivating Nora's deception, the attitudes of Torvald—and society—leave Nora vulnerable to Krogstad's blackmail.

Nora's abandonment of her children can also be interpreted as an act of self-sacrifice. Despite Nora's great love for her children—manifested by her interaction with them and her great fear of corrupting them—she chooses to leave them. Nora truly believes that the nanny will be a better mother and that leaving her children is in their best interest.

PARENTAL AND FILIAL OBLIGATIONS

Nora, Torvald, and Dr. Rank each express the belief that a parent is obligated to be honest and upstanding, because a parent's immorality is passed on to his or her children like a disease. In fact, Dr. Rank does have a disease that is the result of his father's depravity. Dr. Rank implies that his father's immorality—his many affairs with women—led him to contract a venereal disease that he passed on to his son, causing Dr. Rank to suffer for his father's misdeeds. Torvald voices the idea that one's parents determine one's moral character when he tells Nora, "Nearly all young criminals had lying mothers." He also refuses to allow Nora to interact with their children after he learns of her deceit, for fear that she will corrupt them.

Yet, the play suggests that children too are obligated to protect their parents. Nora recognized this obligation, but she ignored it, choosing to be with—and sacrifice herself for—her sick husband instead of her sick father. Mrs. Linde, on the other hand, abandoned her hopes of being with Krogstad and undertook years of labor in order to tend to her sick mother. Ibsen does not pass judgment on either woman's decision, but he does use the idea of a child's debt to her parent to demonstrate the complexity and reciprocal nature of familial obligations.

THE UNRELIABILITY OF APPEARANCES

Over the course of A Doll's House, appearances prove to be misleading veneers that mask the reality of the play's characters and situations. Our first impressions of Nora, Torvald, and Krogstad are all eventually undercut. Nora initially seems a silly, childish woman, but as the play progresses, we see that she is intelligent, motivated, and, by the play's conclusion, a strong-willed, independent thinker. Torvald, though he plays the part of the strong, benevolent husband, reveals himself to be cowardly, petty, and selfish when he fears that Krogstad may expose him to scandal. Krogstad too reveals himself to be a much more sympathetic and merciful character than he first appears to be. The play's climax is largely a matter of resolving identity confusion—we see Krogstad as an earnest lover, Nora as an intelligent, brave woman, and Torvald as a simpering, sad man.

Situations too are misinterpreted both by us and by the characters. The seeming hatred between Mrs. Linde and Krogstad turns out to be love. Nora's creditor turns out to be Krogstad and not, as we and Mrs. Linde suppose, Dr. Rank. Dr. Rank, to Nora's and our surprise, confesses that he is in love with her. The seemingly villainous Krogstad repents and returns Nora's contract to her, while the seemingly kindhearted Mrs. Linde ceases to help Nora and forces Torvald's discovery of Nora's secret.

The instability of appearances within the Torvald household at the play's end results from Torvald's devotion to an image at the expense of the creation of true happiness. Because Torvald craves respect from his employees, friends, and wife, status and image are important to him. Any disrespect—when Nora calls him petty and when Krogstad calls him by his first name, for example—angers Torvald greatly. By the end of the play, we see that Torvald's obsession with controlling his home's appearance and his repeated suppression and denial of reality have harmed his family and his happiness irreparably.

MOTIFS

Motifs are recurring structures, contrasts, or literary devices that can help to develop and inform the text's major themes.

NORA'S DEFINITION OF FREEDOM
Nora's understanding of the meaning of freedom evolves over the course of the play. In the first act, she believes that she will be totally "free" as soon as she has repaid her debt, because she will have the opportunity to devote herself fully to her domestic responsibilities. After Krogstad blackmails her, however, she reconsiders her conception of freedom and questions whether she is happy in Torvald's house, subjected to his orders and edicts. By the end of the play, Nora seeks a new kind of freedom. She wishes to be relieved of her familial obligations in order to pursue her own ambitions, beliefs, and identity.

LETTERS
Many of the plot's twists and turns depend upon the writing and reading of letters, which function within the play as the subtext that reveals the true, unpleasant nature of situations obscured by Torvald and Nora's efforts at beautification. Krogstad writes two letters: the first reveals Nora's crime of forgery to Torvald; the second retracts his blackmail threat and returns Nora's promissory note. The first letter, which Krogstad places in Torvald's letterbox near the end of Act\Two, represents the truth about Nora's past and initiates the inevitable dissolution of her marriage—as Nora says immedi-

ately after Krogstad leaves it, "We are lost." Nora's attempts to stall Torvald from reading the letter represent her continued denial of the true nature of her marriage. The second letter releases Nora from her obligation to Krogstad and represents her release from her obligation to Torvald. Upon reading it, Torvald attempts to return to his and Nora's previous denial of reality, but Nora recognizes that the letters have done more than expose her actions to Torvald; they have exposed the truth about Torvald's selfishness, and she can no longer participate in the illusion of a happy marriage.

Dr. Rank's method of communicating his imminent death is to leave his calling card marked with a black cross in Torvald's letterbox. In an earlier conversation with Nora, Dr. Rank reveals his understanding of Torvald's unwillingness to accept reality when he proclaims, "Torvald is so fastidious, he cannot face up to anything ugly." By leaving his calling card as a death notice, Dr. Rank politely attempts to keep Torvald from the "ugly" truth. Other letters include Mrs. Linde's note to Krogstad, which initiates her life-changing meeting with him, and Torvald's letter of dismissal to Krogstad.

Symbols

Symbols are objects, characters, figures, or colors used to represent abstract ideas or concepts.

The Christmas Tree
The Christmas tree, a festive object meant to serve a decorative purpose, symbolizes Nora's position in her household as a plaything who is pleasing to look at and adds charm to the home. There are several parallels drawn between Nora and the Christmas tree in the play. Just as Nora instructs the maid that the children cannot see the tree until it has been decorated, she tells Torvald that no one can see her in her dress until the evening of the dance. Also, at the beginning of the second act, after Nora's psychological condition has begun to erode, the stage directions indicate that the Christmas tree is correspondingly "dishevelled."

New Year's Day
The action of the play is set at Christmastime, and Nora and Torvald both look forward to New Year's as the start of a new, happier phase in their lives. In the new year, Torvald will start his new job,

and he anticipates with excitement the extra money and admiration the job will bring him. Nora also looks forward to Torvald's new job, because she will finally be able to repay her secret debt to Krogstad. By the end of the play, however, the nature of the new start that New Year's represents for Torvald and Nora has changed dramatically. They both must become new people and face radically changed ways of living. Hence, the new year comes to mark the beginning of a truly new and different period in both their lives and their personalities.

SYMBOLS

Summary & Analysis

Summary

From the opening of the play to the announcement of Dr. Rank's and Mrs. Linde's arrivals.

It is Christmas Eve. Nora Helmer enters the house with packages and a Christmas tree. She pays the porter double what she owes him and eats some macaroons. Her husband, Torvald Helmer, comes out of his study and addresses Nora with tenderness and authority, calling her his "skylark" and his "squirrel." Nora tells Torvald that she wants to show him what she has bought, and Torvald teases her for being a spendthrift. Nora replies that she and Torvald can afford to be extravagant, since Torvald's new position at the bank means he will earn a large salary. Torvald replies that he will not take over that position until after the new year begins. When Nora argues that they can spend on credit until Torvald is paid, Torvald scolds her, reminding her that if something were to happen to make them unable to pay off their loan, they would be in trouble. He concludes by saying that he hates debts because "[a] home that depends on loans and debts is not beautiful because it is not free." Nora finally acquiesces and says, "Everything as you wish, Torvald."

Witnessing Nora's pouty disappointment, Torvald tries to cheer up his wife by offering her money to spend for Christmas. Nora becomes enthusiastic again and thanks him profusely. She then shows him all the gifts she has purchased for their children. Torvald asks Nora what she would like for Christmas, and at first, Nora replies that she doesn't need a gift. It becomes apparent that she is hesitant to tell Torvald what she wants, and finally she says that she would just like some money so that she can pick out the perfect thing and buy it herself.

Torvald again accuses Nora of being wasteful, arguing that wastefulness with money runs in her family and that she inherited the trait from her father. But, he says, he loves his "lovely little singing bird" just the way she is, and he wouldn't want her to change.

Torvald then asks Nora if she has given in to her sweet tooth that day. Nora vehemently denies Torvald's suggestion and continues her denial even when Torvald specifically asks if she has eaten any macaroons. Torvald finally abandons his questions, respecting her word.

The two discuss that evening's Christmas festivities and the invitation of Dr. Rank to dinner. Torvald says Dr. Rank knows that he is always welcome and therefore doesn't need to be invited. Nevertheless, Torvald tells Nora, he will invite Dr. Rank when he visits that morning. Torvald and Nora then return to their discussion of how wonderful it is that Torvald has a secure income and a good job.

Torvald recalls the events of the previous Christmas, when Nora shut herself up in a room until very late every night for three weeks to make Christmas ornaments. He remarks that he had never been so bored in his life. He also emphasizes that Nora had very little to show for all of her toil when she was finished. Nora reminds her husband that she can't be blamed for the cat getting into the room and destroying all her hard work. Torvald again expresses happiness that they are financially better off than they were before.

The doorbell rings and the maid, Helene, announces that Dr. Rank has arrived to see Torvald and that there is a lady caller as well.

ANALYSIS

The transaction between Nora and the porter that opens *A Doll's House* immediately puts the spotlight on money, which emerges as one of the forces driving the play's conflicts as it draws lines between genders, classes, and moral standards. Though Nora owes the porter fifty *øre* (a Norwegian unit of currency), she gives him twice that amount, presumably because she is infused with the holiday spirit. While Nora likes to spend and allows the idea of buying presents to block out financial concerns, Torvald holds a more pragmatic view of money, jokingly calling Nora a spendthrift and telling her that she is completely foolish when it comes to financial matters.

Torvald's assertion that Nora's lack of understanding of money matters is the result of her gender ("Nora, my Nora, that is just like a woman") reveals his prejudiced viewpoint on gender roles. Torvald believes a wife's role is to beautify the home, not only through proper management of domestic life but also through proper behavior and appearance. He quickly makes it known that appearances are very important to him, and that Nora is like an ornament or trophy that serves to beautify his home and his reputation.

Torvald's insistence on calling Nora by affectionately diminutive names evokes her helplessness and her dependence on him. The only time that Torvald calls Nora by her actual name is when he is scolding her. When he is greeting or adoring her, however, he calls her by childish animal nicknames such as "my little skylark" and "my squirrel." By placing her within such a system of names, Torvald not only asserts his power over Nora but also dehumanizes her to a degree. When he implies that Nora is comparable to the "little birds that like to fritter money," Torvald suggests that Nora lacks some fundamental male ability to deal properly with financial matters. Though Torvald accuses Nora of being irresponsible with money, he gives her more in order to watch her happy reaction. This act shows that Torvald amuses himself by manipulating his wife's feelings. Nora is like Torvald's doll—she decorates his home and pleases him by being a dependent figure with whose emotions he can toy.

In addition to being something of a doll to Torvald, Nora is also like a child to him. He shows himself to be competing with Nora's dead father for Nora's loyalty. In a sense, by keeping Nora dependent upon and subservient to him, Torvald plays the role of Nora's second father. He treats her like a child, doling out money to her and attempting to instruct her in the ways of the world. Nora's gift selections—a sword and a horse for her male children and a doll for her daughter—show that she reinforces the stereotypical gender roles that hold her in subservience to Torvald. Nora sees her daughter the same way she has likely been treated all of her life—as a doll.

ACT ONE, CONTINUED

SUMMARY

From the beginning of Nora's conversation with Mrs. Linde to Nora's promise to talk to Torvald about finding Mrs. Linde work.

Nora greets the female visitor hesitantly, and the visitor realizes that Nora does not remember her. Finally, Nora recognizes the woman as her childhood friend, Kristine Linde and remarks that Mrs. Linde has changed since they last met nine or ten years earlier. Mrs. Linde says that she has just arrived by steamer that day. Nora remarks that

Mrs. Linde looks paler and thinner than she remembered and apologizes profusely for not writing three years earlier, when she read in the paper that Mrs. Linde's husband had died.

Nora asks if Mrs. Linde's husband left her very much money, and Mrs. Linde admits that he did not. Nora then asks whether he left her any children. When Mrs. Linde says that he didn't, Nora asks once more if he left her "nothing at all then?" Mrs. Linde says that he did not leave her even "an ounce of grief," but this sentiment is lost on Nora. After commenting how awful life must be for Mrs. Linde, Nora begins to talk about her three children and then apologizes for babbling on about her own life instead of listening to Mrs. Linde. First, though, she feels that she must tell Mrs. Linde about Torvald's new position at the bank, and Mrs. Linde responds enthusiastically.

When Mrs. Linde comments that it would be nice to have enough money, Nora talks about how she and Torvald will have "pots and pots" of money. Nora tells Mrs. Linde that life hasn't always been so happy, however. Nora once had to work as well—doing tasks like sewing and crocheting. Torvald also had to take on more than one job, but he became ill, and the entire family had to go south to Italy because of Torvald's condition. Nora explains that the trip to Italy was quite expensive and that she obtained the money from her father. The family left for Italy at just about the time that Nora's father died. Nora excitedly says that her husband has been completely well since returning from Italy and that the children are very healthy too. She apologizes again for babbling on about her happiness and monopolizing the conversation.

Mrs. Linde describes how she married a husband of whom she was not particularly fond. Because her mother was confined to bed, Mrs. Linde had to look after her two younger brothers. She says she feels it would not have been justifiable to turn down her suitor's proposal and the money that would come with marriage to him. When her husband died, however, his business collapsed, and she was left penniless. After three years spent working odd jobs to support her family, Mrs. Linde is finally free, because her mother died and her brothers are grown. She adds that with no one dependent upon her, her life is even sadder, because she has no one for whom to live. She reveals that she came to town to find some office work.

When Nora protests that Mrs. Linde ought not work, Mrs. Linde snaps that Nora could not possibly understand the hard work that she has had to do. She quickly apologizes for her anger, saying that her predicament has made her bitter. She explains that because she has no one for whom to work, she must look after only herself, which has made her selfish. She admits that she is happy at the news of Torvald's new job because of the implications it could have for her personal interests. Nora promises to talk to her husband about helping Mrs. Linde.

ANALYSIS

Nora's first conversation with Mrs. Linde plays a key role in establishing Nora's childlike, self-centered, and insensitive character. Though she purports to be interested in Mrs. Linde's problems, Nora repeatedly turns the conversation back to her own life with Torvald. Nora's self-centeredness is further demonstrated in her revelation that she failed to write to Mrs. Linde after her husband passed away. It is only now, three years after the fact, that Nora expresses her sympathy; up to this point, she has made no effort to think beyond herself, and the fact that she does so now seems only a matter of polite reflex. Like an impetuous child, Nora does not filter her thoughts, expressing what comes to mind without regard for what is and what is not appropriate, as when she tactlessly comments that Mrs. Linde's looks have declined over the years. Though she recognizes that Mrs. Linde is poor, she unabashedly delights in the fact that she and Torvald will soon have "pots and pots" of money. She does not recognize that such comments might be hurtful to her old friend.

From a structural point of view, Nora, as the drama's protagonist, must develop over the course of the play. Because her first conversation with Mrs. Linde shows Nora to be childlike in her understanding of the world, it becomes apparent that Nora's development will involve education, maturation, and the shedding of her seeming naïveté. Whereas Nora clings to romantic notions about love and marriage, Mrs. Linde has a more realistic understanding of marriage, gained from her experience of being left with "not even an ounce of grief" after her husband's death. Nora's incredulity at Mrs. Linde's remark indicates to Mrs. Linde, and to us, that Nora is sheltered and somewhat unsophisticated. The thread between Nora's initial interactions with Torvald and Mrs. Linde is the tension between Nora's childish nature and her need to grow out of it.

As someone who has experienced an existence that is anything but doll-like, Mrs. Linde seems poised to be Nora's teacher and guide on her journey to maturity. Mrs. Linde recounts hardship after hardship and sacrifice after sacrifice—a far cry from the pampering that Nora receives from Torvald. At the same time, both Mrs. Linde's and Nora's marriages involve sacrificing themselves to another in exchange for money. Nora becomes her husband's plaything and delights in the comforts he provides her, while Mrs. Linde marries her husband for money so that she can support her sick mother and dependent younger brothers. Again and again in *A Doll's House,* women sacrifice their personal desires, their ambitions, and their dignity. While Nora marries for her own welfare, however, Mrs. Linde does so for the welfare of her family.

Unlike many of the dramatists who came before him, Ibsen doesn't portray rich, powerful, or socially significant people in his plays. Rather, he populates his dramas with ordinary middle-class characters. Ibsen's language too is commonplace. Though his dialogue is uncomplicated and without rhetorical flourish, it subtly conveys more than it seems to. For instance, Nora's insensitivity to Mrs. Linde's plight manifests itself when she speaks of her three lovely children *immediately* after learning that Mrs. Linde has none. That Ibsen's dialogue is apparently simple—yet full of loaded subtext—sets Ibsen's drama apart from earlier and contemporary verse plays.

ACT ONE, CONTINUED

> [O]f course, a time will come when Torvald is not as devoted to me, not quite so happy when I dance for him, and dress for him, and play with him.
> (See QUOTATIONS, p. 41)

SUMMARY

From Mrs. Linde's accusation that Nora is still a child to the exit of Dr. Rank, Torvald, and Mrs. Linde

Mrs. Linde comments that Nora is still a child because she has known no hardship in her life. Nora becomes indignant and says that she too has "something to be proud and happy about." She goes on to tell Mrs. Linde that she saved her husband's life when he was sick. The doctors urged them to go south for a while but cautioned that the gravity of Torvald's illness must not be revealed to him—he was in danger of dying. Nora tried to convince Torvald that they should go south, but he wouldn't hear of borrowing money for that purpose. Nora procured money and told Torvald that her father gave it to them, though she really raised it herself. Nora's father died before Torvald had a chance to find out that the money didn't come from him. Nora has kept the source of the money a secret because she doesn't want his "man's pride" to be hurt. Mrs. Linde is doubtful that Nora is right to keep her actions a secret, but Nora replies that Torvald "would be so ashamed and humiliated if he thought he owed me anything."

Nora explains that she has been using her allowance ever since the trip to Italy to pay her debt. She also reveals that she took on some copying work the previous winter. This work (and not ornament-making) was the real reason that she closed herself up in a room during the weeks before the previous Christmas. Nora abruptly shifts the subject from the past to the future and happily exclaims that after the new year she will have paid off her debt completely and then will be "free" to fulfill her responsibilities as a wife and mother without impediment.

A man comes to the door wishing to speak with Torvald. Nora's displeasure at seeing the man is apparent. Mrs. Linde is also startled upon seeing the man and turns away. The man, named Krogstad, has come to speak with Torvald about bank business. Nora tells Mrs. Linde that Krogstad is a lawyer, and Mrs. Linde reveals that she knew him when he was living in her part of the country. Nora says that Krogstad is a widower who had an unhappy marriage and many children. Mrs. Linde replies, "He has many business interests, they say," and Nora responds that she doesn't want to think about business because it is a "bore."

Dr. Rank leaves the study when Krogstad goes in. Dr. Rank and Nora have a brief conversation, and Dr. Rank calls Krogstad "morally sick." He also informs the women that Krogstad has a small, subordinate position at the bank. Nora offers a macaroon to Dr. Rank, who says that he thought macaroons were banned in the Torvald house. Nora lies and says that Mrs. Linde brought them and then explains to Mrs. Linde that Torvald has "outlawed" macaroons because he thinks they are bad for Nora's teeth. Torvald exits his study, and Nora introduces Mrs. Linde to him. Nora pleads with Torvald to give Mrs. Linde a job, and he says that there might possibly be an opening for her. Dr. Rank, Torvald, and Mrs. Linde then leave together, all of them planning to come back that evening for the Christmas festivities.

To be free, absolutely free. To spend time playing with the children. To have a clean, beautiful house, the way Torvald likes it. (See QUOTATIONS, p. 42)

ANALYSIS

Whereas the conversation between Torvald and Nora at the beginning of *A Doll's House* seems one between a happy, honest couple with nothing to hide, in the latter half of Act One we see that the Torvald household is full of secrets and deception. The most minor example of this deception is Nora's lying about the macaroons. Because eating a macaroon seems like such a trivial matter, one can argue that lying about it is highly insignificant. Yet one can also argue that the trivial nature of eating the macaroon is the very thing that makes the lie so troubling. Indeed, the need to lie about something so insignificant—Nora lies twice about the macaroons, once to Torvald and once to Dr. Rank—speaks to the depths of both her guilt and the tension in her relationship with Torvald.

A far more serious case of deception concerns the loan Nora illicitly acquired in order to save Torvald's life. Though this deception is of far greater magnitude than the lies about the macaroons and involves a breach of law (Nora is guilty of forgery), we can understand and forgive Nora for her actions because she is motivated by noble and selfless intent. In both instances of deception, Nora lies because of Torvald's unfair stereotypes about gender roles. If Torvald could accept his wife's help and didn't feel the need to have control over her every movement, Nora would not have to lie to him.

When Nora suggests that Torvald find Mrs. Linde a job, Torvald again shows his biases concerning women's proper roles in society by immediately assuming that Mrs. Linde is a widow. Torvald's assumption shows that he believes a proper married woman should not work outside the home. Also, as Torvald departs with Mrs. Linde, he says to her, "Only a mother could bear to be here [in the house]," suggesting that any woman who wants a job must not have children. These words contain a veiled expression of pride, since Torvald is pleased that his home is fit only for what he believes to be the proper kind of woman: a mother and wife, like Nora.

After Nora reveals her secret to Mrs. Linde, Nora's and Mrs. Linde's versions of femininity slowly begin to converge. With knowledge of her noble act, we see Nora's character deepen, and we see that she possesses more maturity and determination than we previously thought. What prompts Nora to reveal her secret about having saved Torvald's life by raising the money for their trip abroad is Mrs. Linde's contention that Nora has never known hard work. Although Mrs. Linde's accusation of Nora facilitates the pair's reconciliation, what motivates the two women here is unclear. Ibsen does not explicitly reveal whether Mrs. Linde's irritation at Nora stems from envy, annoyance, or even concern. Similarly, Nora's defensive response could signify that she is hurt, competitive, or simply itching to tell someone her secret. All that is clear is that both Mrs. Linde and Nora are proud to have helped those they love by sacrificing for them. Their common experience of sacrifice for others unites them even though they come from different economic spheres and forms the basis for their rekindled friendship.

ACT ONE, CONTINUED

SUMMARY

From the entrance of Nora's children to the end of Act One.

The nanny, Anne-Marie, enters with Nora's three children, and Nora and the children play happily. Krogstad enters and startles Nora, who screams. He apologizes and says that the door was open, and Nora replies that Torvald is not at home. Krogstad says that he has come to talk with her, not with Torvald. He asks whether the woman walking with Torvald is Mrs. Linde, and Nora responds in the affirmative. When Krogstad explains that he used to know Mrs. Linde, Nora tells him that she already knew, and Krogstad says that he assumed that she did. He then asks if the bank will employ Mrs. Linde, and Nora brags that it will because, even though she is a woman, Nora has a great deal of influence over her husband.

Krogstad then requests that Nora use her influence on his behalf. Nora is bewildered, because she does not know why Krogstad's position at the bank would be in jeopardy. Krogstad seems to think that Nora knows more than she is letting on and hints that he thinks the hiring of Mrs. Linde will bring about his dismissal. Suddenly, Nora revokes her earlier claims and denies that she has any influence. Krogstad says that as a bank manager, Torvald, "like all married men . . . can be swayed," and Nora accuses Krogstad of insulting her husband.

Nora assures Krogstad that she will repay all her loans by the new year and asks him to leave her alone. Krogstad implies that he isn't concerned only about the money; his position at the bank is very important to him. He speaks of a "bad mistake" he committed, which ruined his reputation and made it very difficult for his career to advance. Thus, he tells Nora, he began doing "the business that you know about." Krogstad announces that he wishes to rebuild his reputation and to behave properly for the sake of his sons, who are growing up. His small bank job, he explains, was the beginning of this rebuilding of his life and reputation. He then threatens Nora, saying that he has "the power to force" her to help him.

Nora replies that though it would be unpleasant for her husband to find out that she had borrowed from Krogstad, Torvald would pay off the loan, and dealings with Krogstad would be terminated. In addition, Krogstad would lose his job. Krogstad says that Nora has other things to worry about: he has figured out that Nora forged her father's signature on the promissory note. Krogstad informs Nora that her forgery is a serious offense, similar to the one that sullied his reputation in the first place. Nora dismisses Krogstad's suggestion, saying that she should not be faulted because her motives were honorable and pure, but Krogstad reminds her of the law. He threatens her once more and then leaves. The children return, but Nora sends them away. Though she is clearly disturbed by what has just happened, she makes an attempt to decorate the tree.

Torvald returns and mentions that he noticed Krogstad departing. He guesses that Krogstad has asked Nora to speak on his behalf. After some hesitation, Nora admits as much. Torvald scolds Nora for speaking to Krogstad and warns her not to lie to him (Torvald). Nora changes the subject and asks Torvald if he will help her find the perfect costume for the party. Nora asks what Krogstad did to warrant his bad reputation. Torvald responds that he forged signatures. Nora asks what his motives were in the matter. Torvald says he would never condemn a man for one indiscretion, but the real problem with Krogstad was that he refused to admit what he had done and take his punishment. Torvald talks about how lying and deceit corrupts a household's children: "nearly all young criminals have had lying mothers." Torvald exits, and the nanny enters and says the children badly want to see their mother. Nora vehemently refuses, and the nanny departs. Terrified, Nora mutters about the thought of corrupting her children. In the next breath, however, she rejects the idea that such corruption could occur.

ANALYSIS

As Act One draws to a close, we see Nora wrestling with new problems of fear, guilt, and wrongdoing. Her conversation with Krogstad reveals Krogstad as the source of the loan Nora used to pay for her family's trip to Italy. Although the taking of the loan constitutes a crime because she forged a signature to get it, Nora takes pride in it because it remains one of the few independent actions she has ever taken. Nora is also proud that she is able to influence her husband, as she boasts to Krogstad. Nora's boasts about influencing Torvald reveal her desire to feel useful and important. That Nora points out that even though she is a woman Krogstad should respect her influence over bank policy suggests that she senses and fears rejection of her significance on account of her gender. Perhaps she must combat this idea even in her own mind.

Although Nora holds some influence over Torvald, her power is extremely limited. Paradoxically, when Krogstad asks Nora to exert this influence on Torvald on his behalf, Nora perceives his request to be an insult to her husband. Because Krogstad's statement implies that Torvald fails to conform to the societal belief that the husband should be responsible for all financial and business matters by letting Nora sway him, Nora recognizes it as an insult to Torvald for not being a proper husband. Torvald, for his part, believes that Nora is completely useless when it comes to matters of business, but he agrees to help find a job for Mrs. Linde in order to make his "little squirrel" happy. He also shows that he believes parenting is a mother's responsibility when he asserts that a lying mother corrupts children and turns them into criminals, suggesting that the father, while important in economic matters, is inconsequential to his children's moral development.

Krogstad wants to keep his job at the bank so that he can become reputable again, but his decision to gain credibility through blackmail shows that he is interested only in reforming his appearance and not his inner self. Torvald too is preoccupied with appearances, something Nora understands and uses to her advantage. She knows she can put her husband in a good mood by mentioning the costume that she will don at the dance. The thought of Nora dressed up and looking beautiful placates Torvald, who takes great pleasure in the beauty of his house and his wife.

Torvald's remark about Krogstad—"I honestly feel sick, sick to my stomach, in the presence of such people"—illustrates his deep contempt for moral corruption of Krogstad's sort. While he thinks that such a bad character is in direct contrast to his "sweet little Nora," we are aware that Krogstad and Nora have committed exactly the same crime—forgery. Torvald, then, has unwittingly referred to Nora when he scorns "such people." Torvald's unknowing condemnation of the actions of the woman he loves is an excellent example of dramatic irony, a literary device that the makes the audience privy to details of which certain characters are ignorant.

ACT TWO

Something glorious is going to happen.
(See QUOTATIONS, p. 43)

SUMMARY

It is Christmas day. The messiness of the area around the Christmas tree indicates that the Christmas Eve celebration has taken place. Nora paces the room uneasily, muttering to herself about her dilemma. The nanny comes in with Nora's costume, and Nora asks her what would happen to the children if she, Nora, disappeared altogether. Mrs. Linde enters and agrees to mend Nora's costume for her. Nora tells Mrs. Linde that Dr. Rank is sick with a disease he inherited from his father, who was sexually promiscuous. Mrs. Linde guesses that Dr. Rank is the mysterious source of Nora's loan, but Nora denies the charge. Mrs. Linde remarks that Nora has changed since the previous day. Torvald returns, and Nora sends Mrs. Linde to see the children, explaining that "Torvald hates the sight of sewing."

Alone with Torvald, Nora again asks him to save Krogstad's job. Torvald tells her that Mrs. Linde will replace Krogstad at the bank. Torvald says that Krogstad is an embarrassment and that he cannot work with him any longer. He explains that they are on a first-name basis only because they went to school together and that this familiarity humiliates him. When Nora calls Torvald's reasoning petty, he becomes upset and sends off a letter dismissing Krogstad. He then goes into his study.

After Torvald exits, Dr. Rank enters and hints that he expects something bad to happen soon. When it becomes apparent that he is referring to his health, Nora is visibly relieved that Dr. Rank is speaking about his own problem and not hers. Dr. Rank tells her that he will soon die and that he doesn't want his best friend, Torvald, to see him in his sickbed. When the end is near, he tells Nora, he will leave a calling card with a black cross across it to indicate that his death is imminent.

Nora begins to flirt with Dr. Rank, coquettishly showing him her new stockings. She hints that she has a great favor to ask Dr. Rank (presumably she would like him to intervene on Krogstad's behalf). Before she is able to ask her favor, however, Dr. Rank confesses his love for her. This disclosure disturbs Nora, and afterward she refuses to request anything from him, even though he begs her to let him help. He asks whether he should "leave for good" now that he has proclaimed his love for her, but Nora is adamant that he continue to keep Torvald company. She tells Dr. Rank how much fun she has with him, and he explains that he has misinterpreted her affection. Nora says that those whose company she prefers are often different than those she loves—when she was young, she loved her father, but she preferred to hide with the maids in the cellar because they didn't try to dictate her behavior.

The maid, Helene, enters and gives Nora a caller's card. Nora ushers Dr. Rank into the study with her husband and urges the doctor to keep Torvald there.

Krogstad enters and announces that he has been fired. He says that the conflicts among Nora, himself, and Torvald could be solved if Torvald would promote him to a better job in the bank. Nora objects, saying that her husband must never know anything about her contract with Krogstad. She implies that she has the courage to kill herself if it means she will absolve Torvald of the need to cover up her crime. Krogstad tells her that even if she were to commit suicide, her reputation would still be in his hands. Krogstad leaves, dropping a letter detailing Nora's secret in the letterbox on the way out.

When Mrs. Linde returns, Nora cries that Krogstad has left a letter in the letterbox. Mrs. Linde realizes that it was Krogstad who lent Nora the money. Nora confesses that she forged a signature and makes Mrs. Linde promise to say that the responsibility for the forgery is Nora's, so that Torvald won't be held accountable for anything if Nora disappears. Nora hints that "something glorious is going to happen," but she doesn't elaborate. Mrs. Linde says that she will go to speak with Krogstad and she confesses she once had a relationship with him. She leaves, and Nora tries to stall her husband to prevent him from reading the mail.

When Torvald enters the living room, Nora makes him promise not to do any work for the remainder of the night so that he can help her prepare the tarantella that she will dance at the costume party. Torvald begins to coach Nora in the dance, but she doesn't listen to him and dances wildly and violently.

Mrs. Linde returns, and dinner is served. Mrs. Linde tells Nora that Krogstad has left town but will return the following night. She adds that she has left him a note. Once alone, Nora remarks to herself that she has thirty-one hours until the tarantella is over, which means thirty-one hours before Torvald reads the letter—"thirty-one hours to live."

ANALYSIS

Nora's comment to Mrs. Linde that Torvald doesn't like to see sewing in his home indicates that Torvald likes the idea and the appearance of a beautiful, carefree wife who does not have to work but rather serves as a showpiece. As Nora explains to Mrs. Linde, Torvald likes his home to seem "happy and welcoming." Mrs. Linde's response that Nora too is skilled at making a home look happy because she is "her father's daughter" suggests that Nora's father regarded her in a way similar to Torvald—as a means to giving a home its proper appearance.

Torvald's opinion on his wife's role in their home is his defining character trait. His unrelenting treatment of Nora as a doll indicates that he is unable to develop or grow. As Nora's understanding of the people and events around her develops, Torvald's remains static. He is the only character who continues to believe in the charade, probably because he is the only main character in the play who does not keep secrets or harbor any hidden complexity. Each of the other characters—Nora, Mrs. Linde, Krogstad, Dr. Rank—has at some point kept secrets, hidden a true love, or plotted for one reason or another.

Nora's use of Torvald's pet names for her to win his cooperation is an act of manipulation on her part. She knows that calling herself his "little bird," his "squirrel," and his "skylark," and thus conforming to his desired standards will make him more willingly to give in to her wishes. At first, Nora's interaction with Dr. Rank is similarly manipulative. When she flirts with him by showing her stockings, it seems that she hopes to entice Dr. Rank and then persuade him to speak to Torvald about keeping Krogstad on at the bank. Yet after Dr. Rank confesses that he loves her, Nora suddenly shuts down and refuses to ask her favor. She has developed some moral integrity. Despite her desperate need, she realizes that she would be taking advantage of Dr. Rank by capitalizing on his earnest love for her.

When Nora explains that Dr. Rank's poor health owes to his father's promiscuity, for the second time we come across the idea that moral corruption transfers from parent to child. (In Act One, Torvald argues that young criminals result from a household full of lies.) These statements clarify Nora's torment and her refusal to interact with her children when she feels like a criminal. They also reveal that both Torvald and Nora seriously believe in the influence that parents have on their children. Although the children are seldom onstage, they gain importance through Nora and Torvald's discussions of them and of parental responsibility.

In this act, Nora shows signs that she is becoming aware of the true nature of her marriage. When she compares living with Torvald to living with her father, doubt is cast on the depth of her love for Torvald. Nora is beginning to realize that though her life with Torvald conforms to societal expectations about how husbands and wives should live, it is far from ideal.

ACT THREE

SUMMARY

From the opening of the act to the arrival of Krogstad's second letter.

Mrs. Linde sits in the Helmers' house, waiting. Krogstad soon appears in the doorway, having received a note from Mrs. Linde asking her to meet him. She tells him that they have "a great deal to talk about," and it becomes apparent that Mrs. Linde once had romantic relations with Krogstad but broke them off in order to marry Mr. Linde, who had more money. Mrs. Linde says that she felt the marriage was necessary for the sake of her brothers and mother but regrets having ignored her heart, which told her to stay with Krogstad. She tells Krogstad that she wants to get back together with him, to take care of him and his children. Krogstad is overjoyed.

Mrs. Linde hears the music stop upstairs and realizes that Torvald and Nora will soon return. She tells Krogstad that his letter is still in Torvald's letterbox, and Krogstad momentarily questions Mrs. Linde's true motives—perhaps she has promised herself to him only to save Nora. Mrs. Linde calms Krogstad, saying "when you've sold yourself once for someone else, you never do it again." She even tells him that although she originally hoped to persuade him to ask for his letter back, after observing the Helmer household, she feels that Torvald must discover the truth about Nora. The dance ends, and Mrs. Linde urges Krogstad to leave. He says that he will wait for her downstairs, and she suggests that she walk her home. Krogstad then exits.

Excited by the prospect of a new life, Mrs. Linde puts on her coat and prepares to leave. Nora and Torvald enter, Nora begging to return to the party. Torvald compliments and teases Nora for Mrs. Linde's benefit, then leaves the room in search of a candle. While he is gone, Mrs. Linde tells Nora that she has spoken to Krogstad and that Nora must tell her husband everything. Nora says, "I knew," but then says that she will not tell Torvald. Mrs. Linde reminds her of the letter. Torvald returns, notices Mrs. Linde's knitting, and tells her that she should take up embroidery instead, saying that embroidery is a more graceful pastime than knitting. Mrs. Linde says goodnight and then departs.

Torvald expresses his relief that Nora's boring friend has gone, and he begins to move toward his wife. She tells him to stop watching her, but he protests that he is always entitled to watch his "prize possession." He continues his sexual advances, telling Nora that when they are in public, he imagines her as his "secret fiancée" and "young bride." Nora continues to protest, saying she wishes to be alone.

Dr. Rank knocks on the door, annoying Torvald by calling so late. In front of Torvald, Nora and Dr. Rank speak in coded terms about the experiment that Dr. Rank was to do on himself; Dr. Rank says that the result is clear, then exits. Torvald thinks that Dr. Rank is simply drunk, but Nora understands that Dr. Rank has come to tell her that he is certain of his impending death.

Torvald goes to retrieve his mail and notices that someone has been tampering with the mailbox lock using one of Nora's hairpins. Nora blames the children. In the mail, Torvald finds that Dr. Rank has left two calling cards with black crosses on them. Nora explains to Torvald that this means that Dr. Rank has gone away to die. Torvald expresses sadness, but decides that Dr. Rank's death might be best for everyone, since it will make Torvald and Nora "quite dependent on each other." He tells Nora that he loves her so much that he has wished in the past that Nora's life were threatened so that he could risk everything to save her.

Nora encourages Torvald to open his letters, but he argues that he would rather spend time with her. She reminds him that he must think of his dying friend, and he finally agrees that perhaps reading his letters will clear from his head the thoughts of "death and decay."

Torvald goes into the other room, and Nora paces for a while. She throws Torvald's cloak around her shoulders and her shawl on her head. She is contemplating suicide and is about to rush out of the house never to return when Torvald storms out of his study in a rage after reading Krogstad's letter. Nora confesses that everything Krogstad has written is true and tells Torvald she has loved him more than anything. Torvald tells her to stop talking, bemoans the ugliness of the forgery, and calls Nora a hypocrite and a liar. He then says that he should have seen such a thing coming—Nora's father was a morally reckless individual. Torvald blames Nora for ruining his life and his happiness by putting him at Krogstad's mercy.

Torvald refuses to allow Nora to leave and says that the family must pretend that all is as it was before, but he states that Nora should no longer be able to see the children. He says that he will try to silence Krogstad by paying him off and hopes that he and Nora can at least keep up the appearance of happiness.

By this point, Nora has become strangely calm, frozen with comprehension as she begins to recognize the truth about her marriage. The doorbell rings, and soon after, the maid Helene enters with a letter for Nora. Torvald snatches the letter from her hands, sees that it is from Krogstad, and reads it himself. Nora does not protest. To Torvald's relief, Krogstad writes that he has decided to stop blackmailing Nora. In his letter, Krogstad includes Nora's promissory note (the one on which she forged her father's signature). Torvald relaxes, rips up the contract, throws it into the stove, and tells Nora that life can go back to normal now that this "bad dream" has ended.

> *From now on, forget happiness. Now it's just about*
> *saving the remains, the wreckage, the appearance.*
> (See QUOTATIONS, p. 44)

ANALYSIS

For most of the play, we see Torvald delighting in Nora's dependence upon him but not in his control over her. Nora does refer to Torvald's restrictions of her actions—she mentions that he forbids macaroons, for instance—but the side of Torvald we see is more pushover than dictator. He seems to love his wife so much that he allows her to do whatever she pleases, as when he gives her more money to spend after she returns from buying gifts. In the scene following the party, however, Torvald's enjoyment of his control over Nora takes on a darker tone with his somewhat perverse sexual advances toward Nora. He treats her like his possession, like the young girl he first acquired years ago. Contributing to the feeling of control that Torvald is exercising over Nora is that the evening has been of Torvald's design—he dresses Nora in a costume of his choosing and coaches her to dance the tarantella in the manner that he finds "desirable."

Torvald's inability to understand Nora's dissent when he attempts to seduce her stems from his belief that Nora, as his wife, is his property. Because he considers her simply an element of the life that he idealizes, her coldness and rebuff of his sexual advances leave him not baffled but incredulous. He has so long believed in the illusory relationship that Nora has helped him create over the years that he cannot comprehend the reality of the situation—that Nora is discontent with her life and willing to express it.

The hollowness of Torvald's promises to save Nora shows how little he appreciates her sacrifice. Nora expects compassion from Torvald after he finds out about her predicament, especially since, after learning of Dr. Rank's imminent death, Torvald confesses that he fantasizes about risking his life to save Nora's. Once given the opportunity, however, Torvald shows no intention of sacrificing anything for Nora, thinking only of himself and of appearances.

Ultimately, Torvald's selfishness becomes apparent in his lack of concern about his wife's fate, despite the fact that she committed a crime to save his life. He panics upon learning of Nora's crime not because he cares about what will happen to her but because he worries that his reputation will be damaged if knowledge of Nora's crime becomes public. Instead of treating Nora with understanding and gratitude for her noble intent, he threatens and blames her and then immediately begins to think of ways to cover up the shame that she has cast on his family. His proclamation of "I'm saved" after Krogstad's letter of retraction arrives reflects that he has been thinking only of himself in his panic. He says nothing about Nora until she asks, "And me?" His casual response—"You too, naturally"—reveals how much her well-being is an afterthought to him.

Torvald's selfish reaction to Krogstad's letter opens Nora's eyes to the truth about her relationship with Torvald and leads her to rearrange her priorities and her course of action. Her shift from thinking about suicide to deciding to walk out on Torvald reflects an increased independence and sense of self. Whereas she earlier succumbs to pressure from Torvald to preserve the appearance of idealized family life (she lies about eating macaroons and considers suicide—the ultimate sacrifice of herself—in order to conceal her misdeeds), she now realizes that she can exist outside Torvald's confined realm.

ACT THREE, CONTINUED

> *You and Papa have done me a great wrong. It's*
> *because of you I've made nothing of my life.*
> (See QUOTATIONS, p. 45)

SUMMARY

> *From Torvald's attempt to start over after burning Krogstad's*
> *contract to the end of the play.*

Torvald tells Nora that they must forget what has happened. Seeing her face expressionless, Torvald attempts to assure Nora that although she may not believe him, he has completely forgiven her. He says that he understands that her actions stemmed from love and that he doesn't blame her for not understanding that "the ends didn't justify the means." He tells her to rely on him as her guardian and teacher, because he loves her and finds her all the more attractive for her dependence upon him.

Nora changes out of her costume and into everyday clothes. Torvald continues to assure her that everything will be okay. In fact, he argues that, by forgiving her, "it's as if [a man has] twice made [his wife] his own." He says that he feels he has given Nora a new life so that she is now both his wife and his child.

Nora replies that Torvald has never understood her and that, until that evening, she has never understood Torvald. She points out that—for the first time in their eight years of marriage—they are now having a "serious conversation." She has realized that she has spent her entire life being loved not for who she is but for the role she plays. To both her father and to Torvald, she has been a plaything—a doll. She realizes she has never been happy in Torvald's dollhouse but has just been performing for her keep. She has deluded herself into thinking herself happy, when in truth she has been miserable.

Torvald admits that there is some truth to Nora's comments and asserts that he will begin to treat Nora and the children as pupils rather than playthings. Nora rejects his offer, saying that Torvald is not equipped to teach her, nor she the children. Instead, she says, she must teach herself, and therefore she insists upon leaving Torvald. He forbids her to leave, but she tells him that she has decided to cut off all dependence upon him, so he cannot dictate her actions. Torvald points out how she will appear to others, but Nora insists that she does not care. He then tries to take persuade Nora to stay in order to fulfill her "sacred duties" to her husband and her children, but Nora responds that she has an equally important duty to herself. She no longer believes Torvald's assertion that she is "a wife and mother above everything else."

Nora says that she realizes that she is childlike and knows nothing about the world. She feels alienated from both religion and the law, and wishes to discover on her own, by going out into the world and learning how to live life for herself, whether or not her feelings of alienation are justified. When Torvald accuses Nora of not loving him anymore, Nora says his claim is true. She then explains that she realized that she didn't love Torvald that evening, when her expectation that he would take the blame for her—showing his willingness to sacrifice himself for love—wasn't met. She adds that she was so sure that Torvald would try to cover for her that she had been planning to take her own life in order to prevent Torvald from ruining his. Torvald replies that no man can sacrifice his honor for love, but Nora retorts that many women have done so.

Once Nora makes it clear to Torvald that she cannot live with him as his wife, he suggests that the two of them live together as brother and sister, but she rejects this plan. She says that she does not want to see her children and that she is leaving them in better hands than her own. Nora returns Torvald's wedding ring and the keys to the house and takes the ring he wears back from him. She says that they can have no contact anymore, and she frees him of all responsibility for her. She adds that she will have Mrs. Linde come the following morning to pick up her belongings.

Torvald asks whether Nora will ever think of him and the children, and she replies that she will. But she refuses to allow Torvald to write to her. Finally, Nora says that "something glorious" would have to happen for she and Torvald to have a true marriage, but then admits that she no longer believes in glorious things. She cannot imagine them changing enough to ever have an equal, workable relationship. She leaves, and as Torvald is trying to comprehend what has happened, a heavy door downstairs slams shut.

ANALYSIS

Torvald's explanation for refusing to take the blame—that a man can never sacrifice his integrity for love—again reveals the depth of his gender bias. Nora's response that "[h]undreds of thousands of women" have done just that underscores that the actions of Mrs. Linde and Nora, both of whom sacrifice themselves for their loved ones, have borne out. Nora's belief that Torvald should take responsibility for her seems justified, since what she expects from Torvald is no more than what she has already given him.

As Nora's childish innocence and faith in Torvald shatter, so do all of her illusions. She realizes that her husband does not see her as a person but rather as a beautiful possession, nothing more than a toy. She voices her belief that neither Torvald nor her father ever loved her, but rather "thought it was enjoyable to be in love with [her]." She realizes these two men cared more about amusing themselves and feeling loved and needed than they did about her as an individual.

Moreover, Nora realizes that since she has been treated as a child for her entire life, she still is very childlike and needs to grow up before she can raise any children or take on any other responsibilities. Her defiance of Torvald when he forbids her to leave reflects her epiphany that she isn't obligated to let Torvald dictate her actions—she is independent of him and has control over her own life. The height of Nora's awakening comes when she tells Torvald that her duty to herself is just as sacred as her duties to her husband and children. She now sees that she is a human being before she is a wife and a mother, and that she owes it to herself to explore her personality, ambitions, and beliefs.

Mrs. Linde's manner of fulfilling her personal desires balances Nora's. Whereas Nora decides that she must be totally independent to be true to herself and thus rejects her family, Mrs. Linde decides that she needs to care for the man she truly loves to be true to herself and thereby become content. Ibsen positions Mrs. Linde as a foil (a character whose attitudes and emotions contrast with, and thereby accentuate, those of another character) to Nora in order to demonstrate that Nora's actions do not constitute the only solution available to women who feel trapped by society. Mrs. Linde's offer to care for Krogstad and his children will be a positive move for both of them, because they love each other, and Mrs. Linde, having sacrificed her whole life to live with a husband she didn't love in order to help her brothers and mother, will finally be able to live with her chosen partner. Nora, on the other hand, has sacrificed her own will all her life by allowing her father and Torvald to indulge theirs. Ibsen suggests that one finds himself or herself not in an independent life but rather in an independent *will*. Nora exits her doll's house with a door slam, emphatically resolving the play with an act of bold self-assertion.

Important Quotations Explained

1. One day I might, yes. Many years from now, when
    I've lost my looks a little. Don't laugh. I mean, of
    course, a time will come when Torvald is not as
    devoted to me, not quite so happy when I dance for
    him, and dress for him, and play with him.

In this quotation from Act One, Nora describes to Mrs. Linde the
circumstances under which she would consider telling Torvald
about the secret loan she took in order to save his life. Her claim that
she might consider telling him when she gets older and loses her
attractiveness is important because it shows that Nora has a sense of
the true nature of her marriage, even as early as Act One. She recognizes that Torvald's affection is based largely on her appearance,
and she knows that when her looks fade, it is likely that Torvald's
interest in her will fade as well. Her suggestion that in the future she
may need something to hold over Torvald in order to retain his
faithfulness and devotion to her reveals that Nora is not as naïve as
she pretends to be. She has an insightful, intelligent, and manipulative side that acknowledges, if only in a small way, the troubling
reality of her existence.

2.   Free. To be free, absolutely free. To spend time playing
      with the children. To have a clean, beautiful house, the
      way Torvald likes it.

In this quotation from her conversation with Mrs. Linde in Act One, Nora claims that she will be "free" after the New Year—after she has paid off her debt to Krogstad. While describing her anticipated freedom, Nora highlights the very factors that constrain her. She claims that freedom will give her time to be a mother and a traditional wife who maintains a beautiful home, as her husband likes it. But the message of the play is that Nora cannot find true freedom in this traditional domestic realm. As the play continues, Nora becomes increasingly aware that she must change her life to find true freedom, and her understanding of the word "free" evolves accordingly. By the end of the play, she sees that freedom entails independence from societal constraints and the ability to explore her own personality, goals, and beliefs.

3.   Something glorious is going to happen.

Nora speaks these prophetic-sounding words to Mrs. Linde toward
the end of Act Two as she tells her about what will happen when
Torvald reads Krogstad's letter detailing Nora's secret loan and
forgery. The meaning of Nora's statement remains obscure until Act
Three, when Nora reveals the nature of the "glorious" happening
that she anticipates. She believes that when Torvald learns of the
forgery and Krogstad's blackmail, Torvald will take all the blame on
himself and gloriously sacrifice his reputation in order to protect
her. When Torvald eventually indicates that he will not shoulder the
blame for Nora, Nora's faith in him is shattered. Once the illusion of
Torvald's nobility is crushed, Nora's other illusions about her married life are crushed as well, and her disappointment with Torvald
triggers her awakening.

4.   From now on, forget happiness. Now it's just about
       saving the remains, the wreckage, the appearance.

Torvald speaks these words in Act Three after learning of Nora's forgery and Krogstad's ability to expose her. Torvald's conversations with Nora have already made it clear that he is primarily attracted to Nora for her beauty and that he takes personal pride in the good looks of his wife. He has also shown himself to be obsessed with appearing dignified and respectable to his colleagues. Torvald's reaction to Krogstad's letter solidifies his characterization as a shallow man concerned first and foremost with appearances. Here, he states explicitly that the *appearance* of happiness is far more important to him than happiness itself.

These words are important also because they constitute Torvald's actual reaction to Nora's crime, in contrast to the gallant reaction that she expects. Rather than sacrifice his own reputation for Nora's, Torvald seeks to ensure that his reputation remains unsullied. His desire to hide—rather than to take responsibility—for Nora's forgery proves Torvald to be the opposite of the strong, noble man that he purports himself to be before Nora and society.

QUOTATIONS

5.   I have been performing tricks for you, Torvald. That's
       how I've survived. You wanted it like that. You and
       Papa have done me a great wrong. It's because of you
       I've made nothing of my life.

Nora speaks these words, which express the truth that she has
gleaned about her marriage, Torvald's character, and her life in general, to Torvald at the end of Act Three. She recognizes that her life
has been largely a performance. She has acted the part of the happy,
child-like wife for Torvald and, before that, she acted the part of the
happy, child-like daughter for her father. She now sees that her
father and Torvald compelled her to behave in a certain way and
understands it to be "great wrong" that stunted her development as
an adult and as a human being. She has made "nothing" of her life
because she has existed only to please men. Following this
realization, Nora leaves Torvald in order to make something of her
life and—for the first time—to exist as a person independent of
other people.

QUOTATIONS

KEY FACTS

FULL TITLE
A Doll's House

AUTHOR
Henrik Ibsen

TYPE OF WORK
Play

GENRE
Realistic, modern prose drama

LANGUAGE
Norwegian

TIME AND PLACE WRITTEN
1879, Rome and Amalfi, Italy

DATE OF FIRST PUBLICATION
1879

TONE
Serious, intense, somber

SETTING (TIME)
Presumably around the late 1870s

SETTING (PLACE)
Norway

PROTAGONIST
Nora Helmer

MAJOR CONFLICT
Nora's struggle with Krogstad, who threatens to tell her husband about her past crime, incites Nora's journey of self-discovery and provides much of the play's dramatic suspense. Nora's primary struggle, however, is against the selfish, stifling, and oppressive attitudes of her husband, Torvald, and of the society that he represents.

RISING ACTION
> Nora's first conversation with Mrs. Linde; Krogstad's visit and blackmailing of Nora; Krogstad's delivery of the letter that later exposes Nora.

CLIMAX
> Torvald reads Krogstad's letter and erupts angrily.

FALLING ACTION
> Nora's realization that Torvald is devoted not to her but to the idea of her as someone who depends on him; her decision to abandon him to find independence.

THEMES
> The sacrificial role of women; parental and filial obligations; the unreliability of appearances

MOTIFS
> Nora's definition of freedom; letters

SYMBOLS
> The Christmas tree; New Year's Day

FORESHADOWING
> Nora's eating of macaroons against Torvald's wishes foreshadows her later rebellion against Torvald.

KEY FACTS

Study Questions & Essay Topics

Study Questions

1.   Compare Torvald's and Nora's attitudes toward money.

Torvald and Nora's first conversation establishes Torvald as the member of the household who makes and controls the money and Nora as the one who spends it. Torvald repeatedly teases Nora about her spending, and at one point Mrs. Linde points out that Nora was a big spender in her younger days. These initial comments paint Nora as a shallow woman who is overly concerned with material delights. Yet Nora's generous tip to the porter in the play's opening scene shows that she is not a selfish woman. More important, once the secret of Nora's loan is made known to the audience, we see that Nora's interest in money stems more from her concern for her family's welfare than from petty desires. We realize that the excitement she has expressed over Torvald's new, well-paying job results from the fact that more spending money means she can finally pay off her debt to Krogstad.

While Torvald seems less enthralled by money because he doesn't talk about it except to chastise Nora for her spending, he is obsessed with having a beautiful home, including a beautiful wife. He considers these things important to his reputation, and keeping up this reputation requires money. Although Torvald accuses Nora of wasting money, Nora spends her money mostly on worthy causes, whereas Torvald uses his for selfish, shallow purposes.

2. *Why does Torvald constantly reprimand Nora for*
    her wastefulness and foolishness while
    simultaneously supporting her behavior? What
    insight does this contradiction give us into Torvald and
    Nora's relationship?

Torvald perceives Nora as a foolish woman who is ignorant of the way society works, but he likes Nora's foolishness and ignorance because they render her helpless and therefore dependent on him. It soon becomes clear to us that Nora's dependence, not Torvald's love for Nora as a person, forms the foundation of Torvald's affection for her. In Act One, Torvald teases Nora about wasting money but then tries to please her by graciously giving her more. Similarly, he points out her faults but then says he doesn't want her to change a bit. He clearly enjoys keeping Nora in a position where she cannot function in the world without him, even if it means that she remains foolish.

In general, Torvald disapproves of any kind of change in Nora's constant, obedient demeanor because he needs to control her behavior. When Nora begins to dance the tarantella wildly in Act Two, he is unsettled. In Act One, Nora says that it would humiliate Torvald if he knew he was secretly in debt to her for his life, indicating that Torvald wants the power in his marriage to be one-sided rather than mutual.

3.   *Compare and contrast Mrs. Linde and Nora at the end of
      the play.*

By the end of Act Three, both Nora and Mrs. Linde have entered
new phases in their lives. Nora has chosen to abandon her children
and her husband because she wants independence from her roles as
mother and wife. In contrast, Mrs. Linde has chosen to abandon her
independence to marry Krogstad and take care of his family. She
likes having people depend on her, and independence does not seem
to fulfill her. Despite their apparent opposition, both Nora's and
Mrs. Linde's decisions allow them to fulfill their respective personal
desires. They have both chosen their own fates, freely and
without male influence. Ibsen seems to feel that the nature of their
choices is not as important as the fact that both women make the
choices themselves.

Suggested Essay Topics

1. What is the relationship between Mrs. Linde's arrival and Nora's awakening and transformation?

2. In Act One, Mrs. Linde describes Nora as "a child." Is this assessment of Nora's state of development valid?

3. What does Torvald's fascination with beauty and appearances imply about his personality? Do his attitudes change at all over the course of the play?

4. Compare Nora and Krogstad. Are there any similarities between them, especially as far as their relationship to society is concerned?

5. How do the characters in *A Doll's House* use the words "free" and "freedom"? Do different speakers use the terms differently? Do they take on different connotations over the course of the play?

REVIEW & RESOURCES

QUIZ

1. To what country did Torvald need to travel for his health?

   A. Germany
   B. Norway
   — C. Italy
   D. Sweden

2. From whom did Nora borrow money?

   — A. Krogstad
   B. Torvald
   C. Mrs. Linde
   D. Dr. Rank

3. What does the black cross on Dr. Rank's calling card signify?

   A. He is in love with Nora
   B. He is in a bad mood
   C. He is deeply religious
   — D. He will soon die

4. How many children do Torvald and Nora have?

   A. One
   — B. Three
   C. None
   D. Seven

5. Which of the following nicknames is *not* a nickname Torvald uses for Nora?

   A. Squirrel
   B. Skylark
   C. Silly girl
   — D. Peaches

6. Whom did Mrs. Linde abandon for a richer man?

    A. Torvald
    B. Dr. Rank
    C. Krogstad
    D. Her nanny's father

7. Whom did Mrs. Linde work many years to support?

    A. Her dying mother
    B. Her children
    C. Her husband
    D. Her mad uncle

8. How did Dr. Rank get his disease?

    A. He inherited it from his mother
    B. He inherited it from his father
    C. He caught it during the war
    D. He caught from a very ill patient

9. Who helped raise Nora?

    A. Her nanny
    B. Mrs. Linde
    C. Helene
    D. Nora's grandmother

10. What does Nora eat against Torvald's wishes?

    A. Dates
    B. Bacon
    C. Shellfish
    D. Macaroons

11. Where is the play set?

    A. Dr. Rank's study
    B. The Helmer home
    C. Krogstad's house
    D. Mrs. Linde's apartment

12. Whose signature did Nora forge?

    A. Krogstad's
    B. Torvald's
    C. Her father's
    D. Her daughter's

13. What is Mrs. Linde's first name?

    A. Kristine
    B. Diane
    C. Henrik
    D. Hedda

14. ✄ What crime earned Krogstad his bad reputation?

    A. Forgery
    B. Murder
    C. Robbery
    D. Counterfeiting

15. To what does Nora compare herself at the end of the play?

    A. A squirrel
    B. A slave
    C. A prisoner
    D. A doll

16. With whom is Dr. Rank secretly in love?

    A. Helene
    B. Nora
    C. Krogstad
    D. Mrs. Linde

17. During what holiday is the play set?

    A. All Hallow's Eve
    B. New Year's
    C. Easter
    D. Christmas

18. What does Nora do too wildly and too violently for Torvald's taste?

    A. Play with her children
    B. Cook and clean
    C. Dance
    D. Argue with Krogstad

19. How does Torvald learn about Nora's forgery?

    A. Krogstad's letter informs him
    B. Mrs. Linde tells him
    C. He overhears a conversation between Dr. Rank and Nora
    D. Nora tells him

20. How does Nora feel about Dr. Rank?

    A. She thinks that he is boring
    B. She thinks that he is creepy
    C. She doesn't know him very well
    D. She likes him very much

21. What does Torvald tease Nora about at the beginning of the play?

    A. Losing her purse
    B. Spending too much money
    C. Forgetting to do the laundry
    D. Mispronouncing the word "metempsychosis"

22. What does Nora expect Torvald to do when he learns about her forgery?

    A. Take the blame himself
    B. Leave her for another woman
    C. Take the children away from her
    D. Kill her

REVIEW & RESOURCES

23.   What kind of party do the Torvalds attend?

    A.   A birthday party
    B.   A going-away party for Dr. Rank
    C.   An Easter party
  — D.   A costume party

24.   What will be the benefit of Torvald's new job at the bank?

    A.   He will work shorter hours
 —B.   He will earn more money
    C.   He will be able to take more vacations
    D.   He will be able to spend more time at home, taking care of the kids

25.   What is the last thing the audience of *A Doll's House* hears?

 —A.   A door slamming
    B.   A gunshot
    C.   A train whistle
    D.   A dog barking

REVIEW & RESOURCES

Answer Key:

1: C; 2: A; 3: D; 4: B; 5: D; 6: C; 7: A; 8: B; 9: A; 10: D; 11: B; 12: C; 13: A; 14: A; 15: D; 16: B; 17: D; 18: C; 19: A; 20: D; 21: B; 22: A; 23: D; 24: B; 25: A

SUGGESTIONS FOR FURTHER READING

BOYESEN, HJALMAR. *A Commentary on the Works of Henrik Ibsen*. New York: Russell & Russell, 1973.

EGAN, MICHAEL, ed. *Ibsen: The Critical Heritage*. Boston: Routledge and K. Paul, 1972.

GRAY, RONALD. *Ibsen, A Dissenting View*. New York: Cambridge University Press, 1977.

LEBOWITZ, NAOMI. *Ibsen and the Great World*. Baton Rouge: Louisiana University Press, 1990.

LEE, JENNETTE. *The Ibsen Secret*. Seattle: University Press of the Pacific, 2001.

LYONS, CHARLES R. *Henrik Ibsen: The Divided Consciousness*. Carbondale: Southern Illinois University Press, 1972.

MARKER, FREDERICK. *Ibsen's Lively Art*. New York: Cambridge University Press, 1989.

MCFARLANE, J., ed. *The Cambridge Companion to Ibsen*. New York: Cambridge University Press, 1994.

WEIGAND, H. J. *The Modern Ibsen: A Reconsideration*. Salem, New Hampshire: Ayer, 1984.

REVIEW & RESOURCES

SPARKNOTES STUDY GUIDES:

1984
The Adventures of
   Huckleberry Finn
The Adventures of
   Tom Sawyer
The Aeneid
All Quiet on the
   Western Front
And Then There
   Were None
Angela's Ashes
Animal Farm
Anne of Green Gables
Antony and Cleopatra
As I Lay Dying
As You Like It
The Awakening
The Bean Trees
The Bell Jar
Beloved
Beowulf
Billy Budd
Black Boy
Bless Me, Ultima
The Bluest Eye
Brave New World
The Brothers
   Karamazov
The Call of the Wild
Candide
The Canterbury Tales
Catch-22
The Catcher in the Rye
The Chosen
Cold Mountain
Cold Sassy Tree
The Color Purple
The Count of
   Monte Cristo
Crime and Punishment
The Crucible
Cry, the Beloved
   Country
Cyrano de Bergerac
Death of a Salesman

The Diary of a
   Young Girl
Doctor Faustus
A Doll's House
Don Quixote
Dr. Jekyll and Mr. Hyde
Dracula
Dune
Emma
Ethan Frome
Fahrenheit 451
Fallen Angels
A Farewell to Arms
Flowers for Algernon
The Fountainhead
Frankenstein
The Glass Menagerie
Gone With the Wind
The Good Earth
The Grapes of Wrath
Great Expectations
The Great Gatsby
Gulliver's Travels
Hamlet
The Handmaid's Tale
Hard Times
Harry Potter and the
   Sorcerer's Stone
Heart of Darkness
Henry IV, Part I
Henry V
Hiroshima
The Hobbit
The House of the
   Seven Gables
I Know Why the
   Caged Bird Sings
The Iliad
Inferno
Invisible Man
Jane Eyre
Johnny Tremain
The Joy Luck Club
Julius Caesar
The Jungle

The Killer Angels
King Lear
The Last of the
   Mohicans
Les Misérables
A Lesson Before
   Dying
The Little Prince
Little Women
Lord of the Flies
Macbeth
Madame Bovary
A Man for All Seasons
The Mayor of
   Casterbridge
The Merchant of
   Venice
A Midsummer
   Night's Dream
Moby-Dick
Much Ado About
   Nothing
My Ántonia
Mythology
Native Son
The New Testament
Night
The Odyssey
The Oedipus Trilogy
Of Mice and Men
The Old Man and
   the Sea
The Old Testament
Oliver Twist
The Once and
   Future King
One Flew Over the
   Cuckoo's Nest
One Hundred Years
   of Solitude
Othello
Our Town
The Outsiders
Paradise Lost
The Pearl

The Picture of
   Dorian Gray
A Portrait of the Artist
   as a Young Man
Pride and Prejudice
The Prince
A Raisin in the Sun
The Red Badge of
   Courage
The Republic
Richard III
Robinson Crusoe
Romeo and Juliet
The Scarlet Letter
A Separate Peace
Silas Marner
Sir Gawain and the
   Green Knight
Slaughterhouse-Five
Snow Falling on Cedars
The Sound and the Fury
Steppenwolf
The Stranger
A Streetcar Named
   Desire
The Sun Also Rises
A Tale of Two Cities
The Taming of
   the Shrew
The Tempest
Tess of the
   d'Urbervilles
Their Eyes Were
   Watching God
Things Fall Apart
To Kill a Mockingbird
To the Lighthouse
Treasure Island
Twelfth Night
Ulysses
Uncle Tom's Cabin
Walden
Wuthering Heights
A Yellow Raft in
   Blue Water